DMT TRIP REPORTS

EXPERIENCE WHAT IT'S LIKE TAKING 5 MEO DIMETHYLTRYPTAMINE

ALEX GIBBONS

Copyright © 2020 by Alex Gibbons

All rights reserved.

No part of this book may be reproduced in any form or by any electronic or mechanical means, including information storage and retrieval systems, without written permission from the author, except for the use of brief quotations in a book review.

UPDATES

For a chance to go into the draw to win a FREE book every month like our 'Stoner Themed Coloring Book' (below), and other updates on our latest books, subscribe below!

https://psychedeliccuriosity.activehosted.com/f/1

For daily posts on all things Psychedelic, follow us on Instagram @Psychedelic.curiosity

It may be that DMT makes us able to perceive what the physicist call "dark matter" - the 95 per cent of the universe's mass that is know to exist but that at present remains invisible to our senses and instruments.

— Graham Hancock

CONTENTS

Before We Get Started!   ix
A little background on DMT   xi

1. I Tried DMT; This Is What Happened   1
2. The DMT Trip that Altered My World-View   12
3. Third time's the charm; Major breakthrough   26

FAQ's   37
Also by Alex Gibbons   41

BEFORE WE GET STARTED!

As you embark on this journey with us, it's important for us to make it clear from the outset that we are not glamorizing the use of DMT, or any other drugs for that matter. Drugs can be dangerous and the decision to use them for recreational, spiritual, or medicinal reasons, is a personal choice.

DMT is a controlled substance and there may be legal consequences for being caught in possession of the substance in many jurisdictions. It's important that you fully understand this so that you can make an informed decision when it comes to experimenting with DMT.

In all its forms, DMT is a very powerful substance and it should be handled with a high level of seriousness. In case you decide to use it for your own purposes, make sure you do thorough research to avoid unforeseen consequences of using the drug. Take your own health into consideration; if you suffer from a chronic illness, do not experiment with DMT; your curiosity could have life and death consequences.

These stories are for informational and entertainment purposes only. These are first-hand accounts related by people who have tried DMT, however, the names and locations contained herein have been changed for privacy reasons.

You should note that these are the subjective experiences of different people. Just because these people had these experiences doesn't necessarily mean that you too will have the same or similar experiences if you try DMT. Everyone's experiences are unique.

A LITTLE BACKGROUND ON DMT

DMT is short for N, N-dimethyltryptamine. It is a hallucinogen that naturally exists in certain plant species. In South America, civilizations have used this substance during religious ceremonies for centuries. To date, South American natives still concoct a special traditional beverage known as *Ayahuasca*, whose main ingredient is DMT.

Because of its use in religious ceremonies, DMT is commonly known as *the spiritual molecule*, and savvy users have nicknamed it *fantasia* and *businessman's trip*.

DMT is a controlled substance in many countries, although, just like with marijuana, lots of countries and jurisdictions are starting to decriminalize it.

Today, DMT comes in 2 main forms: the kind that's extracted from plants and the kind that's synthesized in the lab.

Plant-based DMT can either be brewed to create a tea-like substance, or it can be crushed into herbal mixtures which are then smoked. Synthetic DMT, on the other hand, often comes in the form of white crystals that can be crushed and snorted, smoked in a pipe, or diluted into a solution and injected. It can also be converted into an oily substance that can be vaped.

1
I TRIED DMT; THIS IS WHAT HAPPENED

This is a report of my experience, tripping on DMT for the very first time. I should start with a clarification: this is not me trying to project some sort of belief system onto the experiences that I had during my trip. I'm just recounting my experiences as they were, as best as I can recall them. I'm not trying to ascribe subjective meaning to those experiences because that'll make them feel less authentic.

My trip

I cleared my afternoon schedule and decided to try out synthetic DMT. In the course of my research on the substance, I had learned that the synthetic kind is easier to acquire (at least in the suburbs of America) and that its effects kick in a lot faster than the plant-based kind.

I hopped onto my bed and I laid down on my back, relaxed. I reached out to my nightstand and picked up my pipe, fully loaded with DMT crystals. I lit it up and took a long drag, first with my eyes wide open. I inhaled as deeply as I could, and I slowly exhaled.

Almost immediately, the room around me turned into some sort of futuristic cartoon universe. All the walls and other surfaces were covered with what appeared to be patterns of eyes.

I closed my eyes and took a second drag off my pipe, repeating the deep inhalation and slow exhalation. This time, my field of vision was completely darkened by my eyelids, but I start to feel as though my mind was being massaged. I could literally feel the tension leaving as my mind loosened up, letting go of all the cramps and kinks. I could feel the fog get lifted, as all the distractions that cloud my mind vanished into thin air.

The effect was surreal, like some heightened form of meditation. It seemed that the DMT had put all my thoughts to rest and my mind was a total blank slate. My stream of thought was completely shut off, and I felt totally present in the moment and very aware of all my senses. It felt as though my brain was being recalibrated in preparation for whatever else I was yet to experience in the remainder of my trip. And yet, as this happened, I felt completely sober; none of my senses were dulled, and I did not feel at all inebriated; if anything, I felt more alert.

As my mind cleared up, three beings slowly emerged from the periphery of my field of vision, and they started to approach me at a sluggish pace. They appeared as though they were made of light, and as I later realized, so did every other creature or entity that I encountered in the DMT world. As the 3 beings got closer to me, they opened up and they started covering me with massive warm blankets that were also made of light. These blankets enclosed in a cocoon and they seemed to radiate the feeling of love into my body through my skin. Suddenly I was completely covered with love and the being started to carry me away, still wrapped in the blankets that they so generously provided.

I was taken into a very mesmerizing museum that was filled with perfectly geometric art pieces. This museum seemed to exist on an extra dimension, one I never knew even existed. I later came to learn that the concept of extra dimensions was well explored both in science and in science fiction, and that extra-dimensional spaces have a technical term: hyperspace.

To understand what hyperspace looks like, think of the world we live in, the environment with which you are familiar, as a 2-dimensional square plane. In comparison, think of hyperspace as a tesseract, an animated one, whose dimensions are constantly shifting. That's what the DMT hyperspace feels like: all the things you see and interact with have an elevated dimension that doesn't seem to exist in real life. In addition to having an extra physical dimension, the DMT hyperspace also seems to have an extra-temporal dimension, as well as an additional metaphysical dimension, which we will revisit later on in this story.

In the museum of geometrical art, I seem to be without a body. I felt like a weightless entity, moving along the museum as a disembodied observer, almost immaterial. As I drifted along in the museum, I noticed that it had caretakers, they were all African, and they seemed to have some sort of familial resemblance. The caretakers took me on a tour of the museum, guiding me along as I looked at the most beautiful art I've ever gazed upon.

At some point during the museum tour, I encountered a seemingly translucent circus performer, who floated up to me, with a giant hoop in his hands. He held out his hoop and lifted it up, and I noticed that inside it, there was a hyper-dimensional masterpiece of geometrical art, one that was much more complex than any that I had at the museum so far. This art-piece seemed to be alive. It ran as though it had an engine in it, and it shook, vibrated, and radiated light all at the same time. The energy from this masterpiece was so vibrant that the circus performer seemed to have a difficult time holding on to the loop that contained it.

As the geometrical masterpiece in the loop started to overwhelm the circus performer, he called out to other beings, who popped up out of nowhere, ready to help. But the circus performer started to say, "I can do this, and he can take it." He repeated the phrase several times, as though he was inviting me to take the hoop from him and assuring me that I was perfectly capable of handling it without much trouble.

"I can do it, and he can take it!" said the circus performer again, this time with a more soothing voice that made me swell with confidence. There was something about the way the entities in the hyperspace communicated with me that felt unusual yet intimate. It's like they could anticipate what I thought and how I felt, and they could talk to me, even though some of them were faceless. And then I realized that they weren't talking at all: They were telepathic, and so was I! All communication in the DMT universe was done telepathically. All the entities there could get into my mind, and I, in turn, could get into their minds as well.

In as much as I enjoyed admiring the geometrical art, and as magnificent and unique as all the pieces were, I got the sense that I should be experiencing something more profound, that maybe I should see a few people, and interact with them, As soon as the thought "I should meet somebody!" formed in my head, I heard this disembodied voice say, "Ah, so, you want to meet somebody?" I could tell from the voice that I was dealing with a feisty being, and I was momentarily startled.

Still, I found the composure to wonder, "Uhm, I don't know, is it cool if I do?" At this point, I had no concept of what counted as "somebody" in the DMT universe, so I was a bit nervous at the suggestion, especially given the sassy tone of the disembodied voice. I heard the same voice beckoning me to come along, so I moved toward a train station that seemed to materialize out of nowhere.

This was no ordinary train station, it was gorgeous, and it was composed of pure light. It had this giant circular door that opened up just as I got closer. I drifted into the circular door and got into the train.

On the train, I realized that there are no carriages; it's a continuous space, and the train looked like it has vertebras. It felt more like I was inside a giant living organism that was somehow also a machine. It moved less like a train, and more like a roller coaster on the wildest loop imaginable. The ride was fun and exhilarating and went on for a long while, yet I had no sense of the passage of time.

When the wild train ride came to an end, I encountered a new group of entities; they were a jovial bunch. They kept cheering me on, and they chanted at me, asking me to shake myself out of my human body. It's like they understood that my old body inhibited me from being as free as they were, and they wanted me to shade it off so that I could be one of them.

I heard them and I felt a strong desire to join in with them, so I started wriggling, trying to shake off my own body, as a snake would shake off its old skin. "Yes! Yes! Yes!" they chanted to the rhythm of my wriggling. I too started chanting along with them as I wriggled myself faster and faster. The more I wriggled, the more ecstatic I felt, and the louder the chanting got. It went on and on, and the momentum got higher and higher, until I felt a sort of climax, as though I had scored the winning goal at a match, and everyone was carrying me up and cheering in celebration.

As the ecstatic cheering subsided, I felt the entities get into my head and permeate my mind. They started opening up these otherworldly glands that were somehow located in my head. I felt my mind expand and open up in ways I never imagined possible. It was as though my head was inflating, accessing new information, and discovering its superpowers all at once.

When my brain's otherworldly glands were fully opened, I recognized my own mind in a way that I had never done before; I realized that all that information, that capacity to conceive cosmic notions, was always a part of me. That the potential to perceive what I had perceived was always in me, only that it lay dormant, clogged like sinuses during allergy season. Now, my mind was wide open, fully aerated, and it felt great.

As my mind inflated and my brain seemed to gain cosmic power, I was fully taken by the beauty and magnificence of the DMT world, and an existential question crept into my mind: How do I reconcile the pain and suffering, the terrible things that happen in real life, with the perfect magnificent beauty of this light-filled hyper-space world? Perhaps this blissful world was detached from the truth; perhaps it was an escape, a curtain over the eyes, a false paradise conceived of wishful thinking.

But even before I could complete that thought, I was thrust

into a dark hellish world, one filled with sadness and death. Suddenly, I was surrounded by shapes that looked like bones and carcasses, and I felt as though rivers of blood were flowing over me, and even through my body. My world was suddenly made up of animal mutilations, death camps, and overwhelmingly sad thoughts.

Oddly, as I delved into the darker parts of the DMT world, I was not at all afraid. Sure, there was a lot of grotesque imagery, and things too sad to describe, but none of it felt scary. It was as though my mind was conditioned to understand and to appreciate the darkness that is characteristic of human nature but not to fear it: fear is a limitation, and in the DMT world, there are no limitations. So, I let the darkness and sadness just flow through me, and soon enough, it all passed and the light came back again.

As the darkness moved to the periphery and vanished, and as the light was restored, creatures of light came along with it. I was visited upon by these massive insects that looked somewhat like jellyfish. They crawled up to me, and they started nibbling away at all the pain and suffering that I endured throughout my human life. They burrowed into me, and they were able to get at even the most profoundly painful experiences that I carried deep in my heart. As they ate my pain away, I felt as though a weight had been lifted off me, bit by bit, until it was all gone.

As the jellyfish insects finished off and started crawling away, I looked in the distance, and I noticed a man. Oddly, he was made of a collection of small black holes, and he sat next to a titanic sized black hole. He had a pensive air about him, almost like a statue, but I could tell that he was alive. I couldn't tell why he was there, and he never came up to me or said anything – he just sat there, lost deep in thought.

Suddenly, I found myself sitting inside some kind of waterfall that was made of pure bright light and awesome love. As the waterfall fell on me and poured through me, I felt this pure unadulterated ecstasy. In the midst of that overwhelmingly fantastic feeling, I had a moment of clarity: I had this clear and irrefutable realization that consciousness and love were the two equally important building blocks of this universe that I inhabited temporarily. The DMT world comprised of complete conscious awareness and love in its purest state, and everything that I saw, felt, or heard in that world, was brought to life by those two components. Strangely, I also felt like I was aware of that fact all along like it was not new information, but a piece of knowledge that was already inside of me, yearning to be understood.

In a quick transformation, my body turned into this vast matrix of perfect fractal patterns. One second I was myself, and the next, I was this beautiful pattern of geometrical shapes. Then I, in my new form, started to vibrate. The vibrations picked up momentum, and I went back and forth, accelerating faster and faster and then it shattered and snapped across the DMT world, leaving behind a ripple effect that felt like unconditional love. At that moment, I had the revelation that I was like a singular beam of light. A light more powerful than the sun. In fact, I realized that I was indeed the actual sun, mighty, energetic, life-giving. It felt like all this time; I had been lying to myself, telling myself that I was something small and insignificant when, in reality, I was the source of all the energy in the universe.

In a fleeting moment, I was an egg. A moment later, I hatched into a cicada. Still, in the next moment, I was levitating upwards and interacting with massive entities I had not seen before.

A little while later, the world went dark, and I got the intense feeling that I was now in the presence of divine entities, the ones responsible for the creation of that world. In the telepathic manner, I had now become accustomed to, they let me in on the core secret of their universe. They told me, "This universe exists so that consciousness can become conscious of itself."

After that, I started to regain awareness of my own body. I gradually forced my eyelids open. I could still see the hyperspaces of the DMT world, now juxtaposed with the real world. It felt like a strange crossover, but I got this strong sense that the hyperspaces were real; that they were always there in our regular world, only that our vision is limited, and we can't perceive them. It's almost like the DMT was a special set of glasses that allowed you to see things and creatures in another plane of existence or dimension, like it was the key to a whole new world, one that was more sophisticated than the regular one.

I remember feeling quite convinced that an enormous part of reality was concealed from us and that I was honored to be among the few that got the chance to see it.

As I was looking around, marveling at the contrast between the two worlds, I thought about my left leg. Now, back when I was still a teenager, I got into a horrible car accident, and unfortunately, I broke my thigh bone. The doctors determined that the bone could not heal on its own, so they inserted a rod through the entire thighbone, which made it possible for me to walk again. I was lucky, and I count my blessings that I didn't end up in a wheelchair, but the thigh bone never felt quite right after that. X-ray images of my thigh show that the femur is just fine, but to me, it always feels weak, stiff, and generally awkward at times. That feeling always bugs me.

So, I had a strange idea: I decided to ask the residents of the DMT world for help with my leg. I shut my eyes again, and I thought, "Can you help?" Almost immediately, I was surrounded by a large team of otherworldly doctors, and they all started checking out my leg, asking me what the problem was, and to let them have a look. They then started, one by one, to turn into beams of light, as they poured themselves into my thigh, right through the flesh and bones.

For the first time in a really long time, my leg felt really great. It was like my discomfort had turned into pleasure. I felt as though a vice grip that had been tightening my leg for years was finally loose. I felt a strong relief that almost brought me to tears. I felt a surge of energy flow from the rest of my body into the leg, and it was as if I was regaining control over the motor functions of the leg for the first time since my accident.

I also felt the traumatic memories from the night of my accident melt away and leave my body, like vengeful ghosts that had finally decided to move on. Filled with joy, I got up from my bed and paced around, thinking out loud, "this is unbelievable! It must be a miracle!"

I was so excited about my leg that I spent the remainder of my trip running around in circles. I stretched my leg further than I ever could since the accident, all the time mesmerized at what I could do.

My DMT started wearing off and I came down quickly. When the high was all gone, I realized that my leg was not permanently fixed; the awkward feeling had returned, and I was as aware of the rod in my thigh bone as I was before the trip. I was back in the regular world, and now all the hyperspaces and telepathic entities were gone. That was the end of my trip.

· · ·

Final thoughts on DMT

I'm not a very spiritual person: throughout my adult life, I have believed in science and not much else. However, I will confess that my secular belief system is slightly shaken after my experiences during this DMT trip. It felt like a deeply religious experience like my mind was opened, and I was made aware of the existence of a reality greater than the one I'm familiar with. It's no wonder that generations of natives in South America and other parts of the world have been using DMT during religious ceremonies for centuries.

2

THE DMT TRIP THAT ALTERED MY WORLD-VIEW

I had been partying all night with friends and strangers after a conference, and it was now three in the morning. I headed back to my hotel room with my buddy Jim and a girl named Sandra. I had scored some DMT, and we were all dying to try it for the first time. Despite the excitement of the night, I had managed to stay sober the entire time, and my mind was fully alert; I was not tired or drowsy, so I don't think any of the things I experienced could be attributed to a tired mind.

In the hotel room, we all took off our coats and sat on the bed. I loaded up a long transparent glass smoking pipe with a few pinches of the DMT crystals, as Jim and Sandra eagerly looked on. Sitting up straight, I put the tip of the glass between my lips, and I held the zippo beneath the crystals in the rounded end of the glass. Soon enough, the crystals started boiling, and small clumps of beige-colored vapor started emerging from the pipe and diffusing in the air above.

I inhaled. The first hit was so noxious that I coughed it out. The smoke was extremely dry and strange, unlike anything

I had ever tried before. I felt like sharp slivers of wood were lodged into my lungs, and they were tearing through my alveoli. I coughed and heaved for a while before I regained composure and returned the pipe to my lips again.

Now that I knew what to expect, I managed to hold the second puff without coughing, and even to go for a third one, before I passed the pipe to Sandra. And with that third drag, my trip started to unfold.

Hieroglyphic symbols and weird geometrical patterns were suddenly all over my field of vision. They filled the spaces all around, and it looked as though they had been painted onto every surface, including the hotel room furniture and the walls. My friends now looked as though they had animated geometrical tattoos all over their bodies, as well as their clothes.

The geometrical images were mostly gold-colored, and the lines that formed the shapes seemed to have a somewhat metallic texture. In a split second, my mind went into overdrive, trying to identify specific shapes in a sea of patterns, like trying to find a needle in a haystack. My gaze would follow a certain pattern, but before I made sense of it, I would be distracted by a more intricate pattern. It seemed that all the patterns were interwoven and that there was a mystical significance to the entire geometrical motif.

I felt that I had an obligation to decipher the sacred meaning behind the pattern, but it just felt overwhelmingly complex. There were triangles, vaguely familiar symbols, pentagrams, and seals. It felt as though every culture and religious tradition – both current and ancient – was represented by at least a handful of symbols and patterns in that vast motif. Even then, the vast majority of the patterns were still totally unfamiliar to me, as if they represented worlds and ideas that were beyond my comprehension.

I was only able to see the hieroglyphic symbols and geometrical patterns for a few seconds, before I found myself being beckoned into one of the symbols, through what seemed like a golden conduit that was beginning to open up. At that moment, it occurred to me that each of the symbols I had seen might have been some sort of portal into a different world, or at least a different time and place. It was like every pattern was a gate that could lead me to a different dimension.

By now, the DMT pipe had gone around the room, and both Sandra and Jim had taken a few drags. Jim handed it back to me, and I took the fourth hit and held it for as long as I could. Prior to this, I had talked to a few experienced DMT users, including my friend Jim, and I had been told that once I saw the symbols, it meant that my journey into the hidden universe was about to start. So as I handed off the pipe once more, I lay flat on the mattress, pulled a pillow under my head, closed my eyes, and tried to relax.

The golden conduit that was beckoning me earlier had now fully opened up, and its entrance took the shape of a funnel. In an instance, I felt myself shoot off through the conduit, like a rocket. As I ascended through the golden tunnel, it felt like I was leaving my body behind, the higher I rose, the more weightless I became, until I was lighter than a feather. Before I knew it, I was like a ghost, fully conscious, but totally disembodied, with the supernatural ability to perceive what mere mortals could not.

The thrill of leaving one's body is almost indescribable. I felt terrified and ecstatic at the same time. Everything that I was – my body, my mind, my brain, and my worries – seemed to vanish into the horizon, and it felt like my soul was getting liberated. By the end of the rise, only a minute part of me still existed, yet I felt whole. I had shed off everything that I was in this earthly dimension, and it seemed that the essence of my being was the only part that could pass through the gateway to other dimensions.

Now in my disembodied form, I spiraled off through the conduit at an incredible velocity. The gold conduit somehow turned into what seemed like a ladder. At this point, I had completely lost my sense of direction. I couldn't even tell if I was moving upwards, downwards, or sideways. It was like I was in space, with no gravity to ground me. The directionless ladder first popped into my field of view from my periphery. It was made of white columns that kept twisting and spinning as I moved past them. The ladder has many turns and curves, and it felt like I was levitating through a tapestry of fractal shapes. I kept accelerating, and the white columns seemed to morph into a continuous curving plane of pearly white plastic surfaces. All the surfaces were gleaming, and vibrant colors started to emerge from my periphery with every spiral turn that I took.

Leaving the spiral white ladder, I was chucked into an extradimensional space that seemed to be made out of nothing but data. The space around was held together by quantum equations that seemed to be beyond the comprehension of any human mind. There were Shamanic symbols spread all over the place, and I had the sense that the realm was constructed by some sort of super-consciousness, one that transcended human imagination.

In the extra-dimensional realm, it felt like all science fiction notions were possible. This was a whole other universe, where natural biological things did not exist. This universe was populated by entities that were light-years ahead of ours in terms of evolution. In comparison to the DMT realm, the real world seemed to be held together by weak entry-level science. It occurred to me that this weak imprecise science might be the cause of all of humanity's problems. Put side by side with the DMT universe; ours was disorderly, inferior, and prone to glitches; that's why we can't coexist, make smart decisions, save our planet.

The DMT universe was an infinite inter-woven pattern of animated mandalas. It was a virtual reality world with countless dimensions. It was like an amusement park from the distant future; complex, fascinating, and difficult to conceive.

I felt an overpowering rush of knowledge flow inside me. I felt like a superhero undergoing a transformation of the mind. This knowledge made me sentient, and as it filled me up, I felt that I truly belonged in the DMT universe. I was convinced that this universe had always existed, hiding in the shadows of my mind, waiting for me to visit it. I consider myself a creative person, but there is no way I could have conceived a fraction of what I saw in the DMT world, so it had to be real. I didn't create it. It existed since the beginning of time, and I was just a fortunate visitor.

I've had vivid dreams before; dreams that felt as real as the fingers on my hands, but I could always tell that they were mere mental projects, creations of my adventurous mind. Under DMT, this was not the case. There was no gap between the reality I was used to and the DMT world. There was no fog in my brain to distort what I saw and felt. This was real. This place existed. Sure, it looked nothing like the physical world, but I did not for one second doubt my reality when I was there.

In a split second, I found myself flying through a maze of patterns and structure, which felt like a vast city.

There were architectural marvels that looked like jewel-plated palaces. In this city, nothing was solid or rigid. Everything was dynamic. I was admiring an intricate cathedral-like building when it suddenly disintegrated and morphed into a skyscraper. Everything was in a constant state of change, so it was difficult for me to store clear mental pictures of the structures that I saw. In the span of a blink, the city skyline would undergo a complete transformation, like one of those time-lapse videos.

I flew over the city at such a tremendous speed that I couldn't remember all the details. I could swear I saw a few humanoid figures waving at me as I swooshed past them. One of them was green in color, and he looked like a giant Buddha. He gave me a nod, then raised his massive hand, and gestured at me as I went along. Some other humanoids seemed to go about their business, oblivious of my presence in their realm.

The DMT city seemed to have geometrically aligned streets, and at all intersections, there were fountains. The fountains were surrounded by revolving mandala patterns that projected multi-colored beams of light in all directions. The fountains looked like the chakra flowers that are depicted in Hindu and Buddhist literature, only they were massive, vibrant, and alive, in a mechanical sort of way.

At the heart of the city, there was one fountain that was much bigger than all the rest that I had seen up to that point. This fountain seemed to nourish the entire city; it felt like it was the source of energy that sustained all the structures around. Instead of water, streams of rainbow-colored energy rays shot out of the main fountain, and flowed in all directions, merging with the structures around. Some of the energy spilled back into the pool below in the form of a frothing purple fluid that seemed to replenish the fountain.

Although the DMT world was constantly transforming, it seemed fixed, at least in its purpose. Everything was made of synthetic material with an artificial glitter, and nothing seemed accidental, random, or out of place. It felt as though the beings and the entities in the realm were busy fulfilling their eternal roles, and they weren't especially preoccupied with my presence there. My visit felt somewhat impersonal to them. I was like a tourist in a foreign land; sure, there were beings that gave me attention when I needed it, but most of them seemed detached and emotionless as if they all understood that they were crucial cogs in the cosmic machinery, and they were not keen on abandoning their posts just to say "Hi" to the stranger drifting past them.

Even as most entities went about their business, ignoring me, I still had a strong sense that we were all connected somehow. Everything in this universe seemed to have the uncanny ability to communicate without much effort. I don't remember any specific sounds from the realm, yet I'm certain that I could hear and understand the thoughts of all creatures in that place. It felt like the beings there communicated through chatters, buzzes, and clicks, yet I could always tell what they wanted, and they too could react just the way I expected them to react.

The DMT world seemed to have some sort of hive brain that could communicate telepathically with mine. The entities seemed to say, "This is real, now you understand". They repeated this phrase over and over as I gazed around with a deep sense of wonder.

At this point, I had been a disembodied spirit for a while, but then I started to regain awareness of my body. Now I could hear myself breathe. My sensations were heightened so that I could feel the air rush through my windpipe into my lungs. I could even picture the air, as though it was a DMT entity in its own right, making its way deep into my chest and supercharging me with life and energy. I could also hear myself swallow. Although my swallowing was involuntary, I felt like the overlords at the DMT world were controlling it.

In fact, all my body functions felt like software programs running on a computer that was programmed by the entities in that dimension; I breathed because they wanted me to breathe, I swallowed because they willed it. I was in perfect harmony with all of them, and felt a profound sense of tranquility, knowing that they were there watching over me.

As I regained awareness of my body, I also became more aware of my immediate surroundings; I drifted out of the DMT world and back into my hotel room. I realized that I was still lying on the bed, stretching around. Although I was no longer engulfed in the extradimensional world of DMT, it was still there, adjacent to the real world. There were golden geometrical shapes, spinning, and changing forms around the hotel room. But as the DMT wore off, so did the patterns, and soon they were all gone. I was back to being myself; only this time, I felt like I understood the secrets of the universe.

Making Sense of my DMT Trip

After my trip, I was convinced that I had been to the spiritual plane. Humans have different notions of spirituality, but they're certain crucial elements that underlie most traditional religions. For example, most spiritual traditions are based on the belief that we are more than just meat and bones; we have a soul that transcends our physical bodies, and it even has the capacity to connect to realms that are unknown or invisible to us.

During my trip, that belief was affirmed in me. When I drifted through the marvelous cities of the DMT realm, I did not bring my physical body with me; instead, I was a weightless entity with the ability to roam freely, to move at supernatural speeds, and even to read the minds of other entities. What could I have become, if not my own immortal soul, with cosmic superpowers?

DMT was popularized in America by Terence Kemp McKenna. McKenna studied the use of natural plant-based DMT in native South American Communities, and he came to the conclusion that western society could benefit from the responsible use of DMT and other psychedelics for spiritual, recreational, and creative pursuits. McKenna observed that there was a world beyond what we could see, a cosmos, if you will, that is only accessible to living souls when they go on spiritual quests. DMT and other psychedelics are traditionally used to catalyze such spiritual quests, and their use is documented across many cultures over the centuries.

I felt convinced that I had witnessed what Terence McKenna had described as the "cosmic giggle." The entities in the DMT universe, according to McKenna, are tasked with the Sisyphean duty of spinning the universe and keeping things functional. As humans, we too have a role to play in that regard. During my DMT trip, I had the chance to peek behind the curtain to see how things really worked.

The DMT universe, I believe, is right next door to our current reality. It's right there, and it's eagerly bubbling, ready to spill into our world. It's hidden in the dark corners of our mind, right behind the line between the consciousness and the subconscious mind. Sometimes, we catch glimpses of it when it drifts into our dreams. It creates the unrecognizable phantoms in our nightmare, the ones we choose to fear instead of taking a moment to understand them. This universe is adjacent to ours, so in those pivotal moments when we really need the strength, it slightly merges with our world so that our "guardian" entities can nudge us onwards.

A DMT trip is perhaps the most powerful, most magical thing that you can experience on this planet, in my opinion. It is awe-inspiring and it can be overwhelming. Once you go on a DMT trip, everything else fades in comparison. Your brain is completely rewired and your belief system is irrevocably overhauled.

Many of us – including me – have bought into existentialism; the philosophical argument that we exist as autonomous individuals with the freedom to choose our own parts, and to act according to our own wills. However, after touring the DMT universe, I realized that this philosophy was deeply flawed. The one fundamental truth of the universe is that everything is connected, and there are forces beyond our comprehension that makes everything function as they do. The greatest irony of my trip was that it opened up way more questions than it answered. It created in me a spiritual thirst that could only be quenched with some more DMT trips.

The DMT trip also bolstered my belief in reincarnation. I felt that we were more than just humans and that at our very essence, we were entities that had the power to bounce back and forth between different realms. In this world, we take the form of human beings, but in the DMT world, we exist, not as matter, but as pure energy and consciousness. It wouldn't be too much of a stretch to assert that when we die, we can very well revert back to this form, and if the universe wills it, we can always come back to earth, perhaps as different people, or even as different life forms.

If we are a part of the vast interwoven tapestry of energy that I saw in the DMT realm, and if we have a role to play, just like the other entities there, then it's not inconceivable that our purpose at this point in time is to be human. Perhaps we are here to learn something. Perhaps we have specific tasks to perform as part of the grand scheme of the universe. Or perhaps our roles in the universe are multifaceted and complex, and we aren't even allowed to see the full picture while we are here on earth. In any case, I'm certain that we are eternal beings.

A while back, I read a book about the existence of a spiritual realm. The author explored a core belief that seemed to link multiple archaic cultural traditions. He had discovered that people from different parts of the world seemed to share the belief that all the places in our physical world has a counterpoint in the spiritual realm. This idea seems consistent with what I experienced during my DMT trip. Although I didn't physically move during the trip, I was, for all intents and purposes, in a different place. A place that shared that physical space, but was totally different, both in form and function. It had to be the spiritual counterpoint that I had read about.

I know a few people who have tried ayahuasca before. Their accounts of the trips they had were significantly different from mine, and that could be because I opted for pure synthetic DMT instead of the plant-based DMT brew. Lots of people who have tripped on ayahuasca tend to receive messages from "nature." They often testify about entities or voices telling them to preserve the natural world, to protect the environment, or to reconnect with the earth. I received no such messages during my trip.

I was not offered any directives or overt instructions by the entities in the DMT world. I was just shown around, and sooner or later, the tour was over. Perhaps spiritual messages are reserved for true believers; for those who trip on DMT in pursuit of answers to humanity's problems, not out of sheer curiosity. The other possibility is that everyone has a different experience, and it's up to the entities in the DMT realm to determine what shall be revealed to each visitor.

I had a strong suspicion that the beings in the DMT world were perhaps the creators of our world. It felt like without them, our world would not exist. To me, it made sense that these beings were parts of a super-conscious entity, like the machines in The Matrix, and we were projections, living in a reality that they simulated, all the while thinking that we were the ones in control. In a way, tripping on DMT was like taking the red pill, and finding out for a fact, that our notions of autonomy and free will are misgiven.

Still, there is a major difference between the entities in the DMT world and the machines in The Matrix. The DMT entities seem to want to help us, and they give us the room to experience life on our own terms, only revealing themselves to those who seek them out.

The existence of the DMT world opens up many other possibilities. To me, it represents a fresh outlook altogether. Since my trip, I've been constantly pondering over some big questions: If there is a DMT dimension, does that mean that there are many other dimensions out there, waiting to be discovered? If such dimensions exist, do the entities that occupy them have influence over us, or do they want something from us?

It seems to me that the entities in the DMT world are way more advanced than us; they are more evolved than we are, and that perhaps, our purpose in life is to try to be more like them. Maybe that was the meaning of what was revealed to me during my trip; that we, as humans, ought to aspire to an existence that is fluid and harmonious.

The DMT world was a sophisticated place, but a peaceful one by all indications. Every entity had a predetermined purpose, and even as things moved at full-speed, there was no hint of chaos. Our world, on the other hand, seems to be built on nothing but chaos; there's death, destruction, and injustice. If we could be even the tiniest bit as evolved as the DMT beings, our world would be a better place.

I'm still puzzled by the synthetic makeup of the DMT world. I had always imagined that if there was a dimension other than the one we occupy, it would have a natural, organic beauty to it. As it turns out, the DMT universe looks like it was designed using precise mathematical equations. There's something mechanical, even robotic about the place. All entities and structures are perfectly geometrical. There is no room for imperfection. Even the humanoids that I saw were made out of precise geometrical lines and arches. What's more, everything was glittery and full of color. By all indications, this world didn't function like ours. The beings looked like they were manufactured in a factory, not born or hatched. I didn't see any plants here, but I imagine even the most symmetrical Christmas tree would be out of place in this world of geometrical perfection.

It occurred to me that this kind of mathematical precision might be the end game of evolution, or perhaps the outcome of a world crafted by artificial intelligence. Maybe that is what it took to exist in a multidimensional hyperspace. The things we do as humans must be puzzling to other less intelligent creatures. Perhaps, in my attempt to make sense of the DMT universe, I'm no different from a dog chasing after a car – I wouldn't know what to do with the facts of that universe if they were revealed to me.

3
THIRD TIME'S THE CHARM; MAJOR BREAKTHROUGH

This wasn't my first DMT trip, but the profound nature of the breakthrough I experienced in the wake of the trip makes it the most interesting one yet. Prior to this trip, I had tried DMT two times before, and on both occasions, I had limited success.

On my first trip, I tried smoking my DMT spice mix in a crack pipe: Big mistake. I burned the herbal mixture, and it produced a horrible tasting, noxious smoke, to which I reacted very negatively. I ended up coughing and gagging during most of my trip, and although I did experience some effects, there was nothing worth writing home about. I mostly had weird hallucinations, none of which seemed coherent. The flame from my lighter seemed to linger in my field of vision, even after I closed my eyes, and before it could morph into something else, I would start coughing again, and I'd be forced to open my eyes.

My second trip wasn't that fruitful either, although it was a lot more meaningful than my first one. I wasn't going to make the same mistake twice, so in place of a crack pipe, this time I got myself a decent glass dab rig. I had shared my crack pipe predicament on an Internet forum, and the members were nice enough to let me know that the dab rig would refine the smoke and make it less noxious.

Still, I was overwhelmed by memories of the negative experience I had the first time around, so I sort of chickened out. I only took a couple of shallow puffs, and then I stopped smoking altogether. I have always been a lightweight when it comes to using mind-altering substances, so I thought those shallow drags would suffice, but they didn't.

Instead of a full-on trip, I had a brief auditory hallucination, where I felt as though I was in a white landscape, covered with snow. This was a very serene and isolated place. I later came to realise that this auditory hallucination represented my heart; it was my rhythmic heartbeat that created the vast monochromatic auditory landscape that I inhabited for those few minutes. My second trip ended almost as soon as it began, and although I didn't get much out of it, at least I was able to dispel the negative notions about DMT that I got from my maiden trip. It gave me the confidence to try DMT for the third time, and as you'll see, I'm glad I did.

My breakthrough trip

As I was setting things up for my third DMT trip, I couldn't help but feel a little nervous. After two unsatisfactory experiences, I had a lot riding on this trip, and I had every intention of going all the way on this one. I was neither afraid nor hesitant, just a bit anxious.

I intended to make my DMT trip as authentic as possible, so I decided to incorporate aspects of native South American culture into it. I put my dab rig next to my computer on the desk, and I hit "Play" on a video that was paused on my monitor.

I had spent most of the evening searching online for music videos that were shot during Shamanic ayahuasca ceremonies. In Central and South America, ayahuasca, a brew containing DMT, is used in religious ceremonies, as part of a cultural practice that dates back centuries. Thanks to the recent rise in popularity of DMT around the world, people have been sharing videos related to these ceremonies online. I had gone through a number of interesting videos, and I had settled on a particularly interesting one. It was a medley of traditional songs, recorded by tribesmen from the Peruvian Amazonia region.

I put on my headphones and listened to music for a while. I felt that in order for my experience to be authentic, I had to get in the right mood; to imagine myself, dancing around vigorously with those tribesmen, in a clearing somewhere in the Amazon.

After a while, I felt good and ready. I paused the music and picked up my dab rig. I lit up my torch, and I held the dab rig to my mouth. I heated up the DMT spice mix, and in no time, cloudy white vapors started to rise up the rig and into the inhalation tube.

I took the first hit. This time, I resolved that I would not be deterred by anything, so, despite the strong urge to cough, I took a long drag, held it in my lungs for as long as I could. I then released it slowly through my nose with my lips closed tight, and with my hand over the dab rig mouthpiece to keep the precious vapors from escaping.

I put the rig back onto my lips for a second hit. This time, I decided I would keep breathing the vapor, and my lips would only leave the rig when all the vapor was gone, or when I was too woozy to keep holding it.

I kept breathing the vapor, and in a short while, I felt myself starting to drift off. I was holding the bong in my hand as tightly as I could, but somehow, I felt as though it was getting away from me, as though my hands were no longer a part of me, and it was someone else carrying the dab rig, slowly taking it away. Then, there was a ringing sound in my ears. The strange thing was the ringing seemed to come from within my head.

I kept inhaling and exhaling the vapor. As the DMT started taking effect, the sensation of the vapor in my lungs changed somewhat. It stopped feeling like a vapor, and it now felt like a warm channel of gold-colored energy, rushing into my lungs, charging me with superhuman strength. Only a moment before, I had been afraid to take those hits, but now it felt like the greatest thing in the world. I continued taking the hits until I was afraid I would totally lose motor control or the physical awareness of my hands. At this point, I put the dab rig on the desk.

I gazed at my computer monitor. I paused the music video I was playing earlier, and there was an image of the jungle on the screen. As I stared at that image, something strange happened. The image slowly covered my entire field of vision, all the way to the periphery, and the image suddenly became animated. Somehow, my mind assumed that I was there, physically present in the jungle. It was as though I had jumped into the screen, and come out on the other side, in a different continent, taking part in a ritual whose spiritual significance I had not yet fully grasped.

I tried to move my gaze from the screen to the other parts of my room, to see if the jungle hallucination would go away, but it didn't. Instead, the walls in my room started to pulsate and break apart. One second they were solid walls, and the next, they broke away, and in their place, there were trees, shrubs, and vines all over the place.

Now my entire body started to get disconnected. The cells in my abdominal area felt like they were disintegrating into free atoms, flying away by the millions with each passing second; at least that's how I pictured it in my mind. I knew what was coming next; I had done enough research about DMT to know that I was about to lose awareness of my body, so, when I still could, I dragged myself off the desk, sat on my bed, and lay down flat on my back.

I closed my eyes, and instead of the darkened field of vision that I'm used to, there was a myriad of colored architectural components overlaying the dark background. The architectural components kept re-aligning themselves until they formed a magnificent, giant room. The room was unlike any I had ever seen or even imagined. It was very real, very vivid. Its components were three dimensional, and I seemed to be moving around in it. At this point, I was very excited because I knew my trip was going well this time around.

In that excitement, I thought to myself, "I did it!"

Out of nowhere, a cartoonish teddy bear popped up in front of me and yelled, "You did it!" He seemed to be either matching or exceeding my level of enthusiasm as if my success was somehow also his success. He had this nice outfit on, and he hopped around excitedly. He offered me a joyous greeting, and he seemed to know everything that I was thinking and feeling. When a thought popped into my mind, he would say it out loud, almost immediately, for instance, I thought to ask him, "how are you doing?" but he asked me the question instead, just as the thought was taking form.

The cartoon bear waved his massive paw and threw sparkling glitter and flower petals on the path ahead of me, and he beckoned me to follow him, I floated next to him for a while. As he excitedly kept lining my path with sparkles, I realized that he was leading me towards a grand door that had materialized on one side of the room. I started getting curious. When we got to the door, the teddy bear faced the door with his back towards me and lifted both of his arms up in the air. The massive door split in the middle, and both sides slowly spread themselves wide open. The strange thing is that they opened to reveal a room that was just as dark as the one we were in.

The bear stepped aside and I noticed that there was a big lock in the middle of the doorway; instead of the lock moving along with the opening doors, it stayed suspended in place, and it started to spin and change shape. It was gold-colored and it emitted rays of light as it spun. It kept spinning and growing in size, and it instantly burst open and turned into some sort of animated ring with a dark portal on the inside. It became apparent to me that the teddy bear wanted me to go in through that portal. "You won't like this but it's okay," the bear said as he signaled me to go in.

I felt at that moment that I could trust the bear, so I conjured a smile and repeated the last part of what the bear had said: "It's okay."

I walked – more like drifted – into the portal, and the darkness seemed to disappear as I moved through it. I immediately found myself in a different scene altogether. I was in what seemed like an open space, and on the horizon, there was a bright source of light that reminded me of the sun. As the source of light came into focus, I noticed that it had petals around it, sort of like a golden flower that was in the process of opening up. I thought the image looked familiar at the moment, but I couldn't place it. Later, after my trip, I remembered where I had seen it before: It was the symbol of the seventh chakra (also known as the crown chakra), as depicted in Hindu and Buddhist literature. In eastern religions, the crown chakra is believed to be a special "energy center" that is located at the top of the head, and it's responsible for our spiritual connection with nature and the universe.

The glowing image of the crown chakra moved towards me, but as it got closer, its bright colors faded, and it transformed into an outline that looked like a long dark corridor. The corridor seemed to pulsate, and inside it, I noticed that there was an animated male humanoid. This entity looked like a dark figure that was made of geometrical lines. Since the corridor was mostly dark, the humanoid didn't seem to have well-defined details.

The most memorable detail about him was that he had an aura around his entire body. The aura was made up of a wide assortment of vibrant colors. However, despite the colorful nature of aura, I could tell that it had a troubled feel to it. Somehow, I knew that the aura lacked balance, and it was struggling to center itself. It would pulsate in an irregular rhythm, changing color from random brighter shades, to sad darker shades.

I don't know how, but somehow, I just knew what this was about. I could tell that the dark humanoid figure represented me. I had the sense that I was being guided by an invisible entity. I couldn't see that entity, but I could feel its presence lingering over me. I knew that the entity was in control of the environment that I was in at the moment. The entity, I believe, was some sort of spiritual warden of the DMT world, and it had some business with me. It created the reality that I inhabited because it needed to show me something.

But just as I was starting to make sense of the presence and role of the spiritual warden and the DMT version of myself, I realized that we had company. In the periphery of my eyes, I noticed a very dark entity, just standing there, waiting for a chance to seize control over my vision. This entity unsettled me a bit because I could tell that it didn't have the best intentions for me, but with the spiritual warden watching over me, I still felt safe.

I decided to ignore the dark entity in my periphery, but I could tell that it was displeased. It wanted me to pay attention to it. It tried to take a more intimidating stance, but I instead chose to wrap myself in the warmth of the spiritual warden entity and focus on whatever message it had for me.

"That's you!", I heard the spiritual warden say to me telepathically, as I shifted my attention back to the humanoid with the sad aura. I scrutinized the humanoid, and I noticed a shift in its aura. The aura started to move upwards and concentrate around the head, forming a halo that was made of golden light. The halo also started to flicker as the aura had done, shifting between bright gold and dark grey.

The humanoid reached out one of his hands into the dark corridor behind him, and he held on to something. My gaze followed his hand to see what he was trying to catch. I realized that he was reaching out towards this elusive feminine energy. I immediately understood what this was about.

The feminine energy was definitely my ex-girlfriend. We had a tumultuous relationship, and we broke up a few months ago. That had been a constant source of pain and regret for me because I truly believed that she was my soulmate; that she and I were written in the stars. In retrospect, I think the relationship was doomed to fail because we both got into it with a lot of baggage. We each had deep-seated issues, and we fought constantly. In the end, we sabotaged the relationship, and in its aftermath, I was thrown into a deep depression. I came very close to giving up on life. I would have given anything to get things back to the way they were before.

Yet, in the middle of my DMT trip, there she was. Not in her physical form, but as this distinctly feminine energy. The spiritual warden focused my attention on the hand of the humanoid that represented me.

That's when it all came together. I noticed that as the hand opened up and released my ex-girlfriends energy, the darkness would slowly vanish, my aura would be colorful, and my halo would turn into a bright golden light. But just as my aura and halo were starting to glow, my hand would reach out and grasp onto my ex-girlfriend's energy again. As I did that, my aura and halo would turn dark once more.

The DMT version of me kept doing the same thing over and over, and the cycle kept repeating itself. I realized this had been the intention of the spiritual guide all along; to show me the reason for the imbalance in my aura, which I believe represents my emotional and mental state.

At that moment, I also had the realization that the spiritual warden had the ability to control the humanoid that represented me. Since it was the creator of this world, it had power over everything in it. I knew this because it allowed me to know it. It had a reason for bestowing me with that knowledge. It wanted to hand over control of my humanoid representative to me so that I could control myself!

When the spiritual warden gave me control over the humanoid, I could immediately feel the colors of my aura and halo synchronize with my emotional state. I thought about my breakup. I felt pain and guilt over what had happened, and the aura around my humanoid representative turned into a dark glow. When I felt sad, the halo turned into a cloudy dark-grey color. By all indications, the aura and halo around the humanoid were visual indicators of my changing emotions.

I tried to summon all the strength that I could so as to let go, once and for all, but I failed. My emotions swung back and forth, and as a result, the aura around the humanoid just kept flickering. As difficult as the moment was, I couldn't help but be amazed by the visual beauty that resulted from my emotional turmoil. The flickering halo had turned into something mesmerizing. It was as though the humanoid was doing an interpretive dance based on my feelings. He wasn't mocking me; he was turning my conflicted emotions into visual art.

I realized at that moment that my pain, guilt, and sadness weren't necessarily bad things. I felt that I needed to accept the fact that they were a part of life; and that there was something beautiful, wholesome and life-affirming about those feelings. I released my ex-girlfriend's energy once more, and this time, I didn't feel the overwhelming urge to reach out and grab it again. Instead, I felt a profound sense of relief.

Just as the feminine energy drifted away, my aura and my halo turned into pure bright light. The light expanded and covered most of my visual field, and I could feel a warmth spreading around, chasing away the darkness, and embracing me. I moved towards my humanoid representative, and somehow, we merged into one and turned into a blob of pure energy and light.

I felt the DMT start to wear off, so I tried to bask in the warmth for a while. I could sense the spiritual warden drifting away, and he bid me a telepathic farewell. I opened my eyes, and the golden light of the DMT realm slowly vanished away, as my room came back into focus.

After the DMT was completely worn off, I realized that I was still happy and tranquil. I really had let go of my sadness, anger, and guilt, and I felt ready to open myself up to a world of new possibilities.

FAQ'S

Can you die from taking DMT?

When DMT is taken in extremely high dosages, it can result in serious side effects (which may include cardiac events, seizures, or a coma) that may end in death. However, in most documented cases where death was connected with the use of DMT, it is usually the case, that DMT was mixed with other strong drugs, or that the user had a serious underlying medical condition that contributed to his or her death.

So, while extremely high doses of DMT may be lethal, a healthy person who uses a moderate amount of DMT without mixing it with other drugs is not likely to die as a result of the recreational use of the psychedelic.

It's also important to note that DMT has been known to cause vomiting, especially among first time users. In itself, vomiting is not necessarily a dangerous thing. However, when you are high, it can be a problem because you might not have the presence of mind to lean over as you throw up. As a result, you run the risk of asphyxiation (choking on your own vomit), which could result in death.

As a precaution, to reduce the risk of asphyxiation, you can have a friend keep an eye on you as you try out DMT.

Does DMT smell?

In its herbal form, DMT has a unique floral smell that is somewhat acrid. DMT crystals on the other hand tend to smell like new sneaker shoes, or rubber. Some users have pointed out that it smells a bit like a new car.

When DMT is burnt, it has a similar smell as burning plastic, although it's a lot more noxious. The smell of burning DMT is so strong that even experienced smokers (those who are used to cigarettes and marijuana) often find themselves coughing. Some users have described the smell as a mixture of burning plastic and rotting carcasses.

Although DMT has a very strong smell, it doesn't linger around for more than a couple of days. You might still want to avoid smoking it in common areas as other people may find it off-putting.

As a point of caution, avoid ingesting DMT that smells like spirit, lighter-fluid or naphtha (moth balls). When you come across DMT that has such smells, it means that it was extracted using a sloppy chemical process, and it may contain dangerous chemicals that could be harmful to your health.

What does a bad trip feel like?

You are likely to experience a bad DMT trip if you mix your DMT with other substances (e.g. marijuana), if you smoke an unusually high dosage, or if you go into your trip with a "dark" mindset. According to many DMT users, a bad trip can be violent and scary, or you can get stuck in some sort of loop.

When you are stuck in a loop, it means that your experience, vision or hallucination is being repeated and you don't seem to get anywhere on your trip. For example, you can see the same pattern for the entire duration of your trip, or you can see a series of patterns that keep changing, only for them to come back over and over again.

Scary DMT trips often involve being haunted or tormented by the entities in your DMT vision. You might feel as though you are being chased or threatened by both visible and invisible entities. You might hear sounds such as maniacal laughter, which can be very unsettling.

Instead of experiencing pleasurable bursts of energy running through you, on a bad trip you might feel as though you are being shocked, scratched, poked, or even stabbed.

You might also feel as though the entities are manipulating you; planting ideas that you dislike into your mind. It might also feel as though some of your life's worst fears are coming true. Your sense of time may also be distorted, and you might feel like you are spending a very long time in a scary universe you hardly recognize. You may regain enough awareness to start wishing that your trip was over, but if this happens, you will be stuck in limbo, until the DMT wears off.

You could try using a moderate dosage of unadulterated DMT and thinking positive thoughts right before your trip to reduce the chances of a bad trip. However, even then, it's a coin-toss, and your trip could turn out to be either good or bad, whether you like it or not.

The worst case scenario for a bad DMT trip is ending up

in a coma where you experience terrifying psychedelic dreams for a long time.

How long does a bad trip last?

A bad trip usually has the same duration as a good trip; somewhere between five and twenty minutes. However, if the bad trip is the result of mixing DMT with other substances, it can last a bit longer than that.

A bad trip that results from drinking the ayahuasca brew can last up to about six hours.

What is ego death on DMT?

Ego-death is a psychology term that refers to the total loss of subjective self-identity. In DMT (and in the use of other psychedelics), it refers to a situation whereby you lose your sense of self.

When you experience ego-death during your trip, you feel like your body is not there anymore, as though your mind is the only part of you that exists, and it is able to move freely through a spiritual universe.

Ego-death also feels like you have no control over what happens to you; you feel like you are adrift in a place that is controlled by other entities, and you have no mastery over your environment. Things just spin and swirl around. You are fully awake, yet you have no sense of personal identity.

You also feel like you are more than just human; like there is a part of you that lives on even when your body is gone. That's why many DMT users who self-identify as atheists often end up acknowledging that there is a spiritual component to the use of the psychedelic.

ALSO BY ALEX GIBBONS

Did you enjoy the book or learn something new? It really helps out small publishers like Alex if you could leave a quick review on Amazon so others in the community can also find the book!

Want to chill and experience the benefits of mindfulness? Want to do something productive while watching random videos on YouTube?

Get this fun stoner themed coloring book to scribble on for your next trip. Search for 'Alex Gibbons Stoner Coloring Book' on Amazon to get yours now!

Thinking about taking other magical drugs? Ever wondered what exactly happens when you take them? Want to make sure you don't have a bad trip?

If you want to read more about the history, origins and effects of Magic Mushrooms, LSD/Acid or DMT, search for 'The Psychedelic Bible' on Amazon!

For daily posts on all things Psychedelic, follow us on Instagram @Psychedelic.curiosity

www.ingramcontent.com/pod-product-compliance
Lightning Source LLC
Chambersburg PA
CBHW071757080526
44588CB00013B/2279